"Stop Yelling And Love Me More, Please Mom!"

Positive Parenting Is Easier Than You Think

With Bonus Book: **Love Him More! Keep Your Relationship Strong After Having A Baby**

Jennifer N. Smith

Copyright © 2016 Jennifer N. Smith

All rights reserved.

ISBN:1530676657

ISBN-13: **978-1530676651**

CONTENTS

"Stop Yelling And Love Me More, Please Mom!"

1	It's Been a Rough Day	1
2	Be a Bully and You will Raise a Bully	4
3	Peaceful Parent, Peaceful Child	9
4	Positive Parenting in Action	13
5	Positive Parenting From Day One	18
6	Terrific Twos and Beyond	20
7	The Magic Years	23
8	Oh the Places They Will Go, Like School	26
9	Is it Time for "The Talk"	29
10	Where Did My Happy Child Go?	32
11	My Baby is All Grownup	34
12	Tips to be a more Positive Parent and stop that " YELLING"	37

1 IT'S BEEN A ROUGH DAY

The kids woke up late and missed the bus for school. One of them couldn't find his homework. On the way out the door the other one informs you that she needs one dozen cupcakes for a class party. Frustrated, you find yourself yelling at them all the way to school. **Now everyone's day is off to a bad start.**

For many parents this is a typical morning. We are faced with countless demands from our kids, our boss and sometimes even our partners. Most of us feel frustrated and unappreciated. No wonder we resort to screaming and yelling. But it doesn't need to be this way.

Like most parents whose day starts this way, you often spend the workday feeling guilty. You didn't mean to say the things you did that made your children cry. You promise yourself that when you get home you will make it up to them. Maybe you decide to pick up their favorite meal and spend some quality time with the kids while you eat.

When you get home from work that idea goes straight out the window. The house is in chaos. Neither their homework nor their chores have been done. Instead of sitting down to dinner you now have to wash the dishes and clean the house first. **And then what happens? Frustration rears its ugly head and the yelling begins again.** Let's face it, being a parent is hard. No matter how many books you read during pregnancy, nothing prepares you for the day to day work involved with raising children. More often than not, our parenting style is a reflection of how we were raised as children. If your parents were strict and yelled a lot, that is likely to be your parenting style as well. Many parents believe that yelling is the only way to get their child's attention. They wrongly assume that yelling doesn't hurt them after all. But our yelling scares children. When they are scared of us they automatically tune us out. Our anger can drive them away and destroy any kind of loving connection we have made.

Yelling at our kids triggers the "fight or flight" mechanism. The child does not hear what you are saying when in this heightened state of being. All they know is that they are scared. You are also teaching your kids to only respond to you when your voice is raised.

Unfortunately, this type of parenting does not benefit you or your child. You cannot raise a happy child if you are constantly screaming threats at them. No parent sets out to hurt their child but this type of parenting does just that.

To raise a happy child that wants to behave you need to retrain yourself first. You need to change the way you think and react to their behavior.

Reading this book is a great place to start. **In the following chapters, you will see why strict and permissive parenting do not work. You will learn just how easy it is to embrace a positive parenting style. While learning how to be a positive parent,** you will not only heal the relationship with your children, but heal yourself along the way.

The first step is knowing what to expect at each of the developmental stages of childhood. As parents we often make the mistake of thinking that our children should just **"know better"**. Not true. As grownups, it is our job to know better. In each chapter of this book you will learn positive parenting tips that work for the developmental stage of your child.

Making the decision to be a positive parent will benefit your whole family. You will find that your children want to behave and follow your rules. You will be less stressed out by the end of the day.

Your house will not feel like a battle zone. Instead you can create a home full of peace and love for the whole family.

2 BE A BULLY AND YOU WILL RAISE A BULLY

For years, there have been two types of parents, strict or permissive. Your own parents probably fell into one of these categories. But study after study has shown us that these styles do not work to raise happy kids that love us and do well in every aspect of their life.

Strict parents that use threats and intimidation to make their children behave tend to raise aggressive, unhappy children. While the opposite, permissive parents, end up with children who are rebellious and constantly pushing the edges of the envelope. If you fall into one of these two categories, continue reading to learn why these methods do not work.

- **Strict Parenting**

Many people believe that being a strict parent will make their children better behaved. After all, it makes sense that your child will not break your rules if they know they will be punished for doing so. No one wants to be spanked or put in time out.

But this parenting style is old fashioned and outdated. Developing a loving relationship with your child cannot be done with fear and intimidation. If you bully your child into listening to you, you will only raise a bully in return. Being an authoritarian parent does not help your child to grow and mature into a productive adult.

This parenting style can actually create more problem behaviors than it curbs. Studies have shown that children with strict parents have lower self-esteem, more aggressive behavior and **often become excellent liars.** Children need to be able to learn how to control their impulses and moderate their feelings. By doing so they learn self-discipline that should be the goal of every parent.

Setting harsh limits teaches your child that they are not responsible for their actions. These limits may make your child behave today, but will not help them to learn the self-discipline needed to control their behavior later in life. In most cases, your child will be very well behaved when you are around, but get into trouble when you are not.

Children model the behavior they see around them. **If you yell at your child in turn they will yell at their peers.** If you bully them into being good, they will in turn bully others to get what they want. Using forms of physical discipline, like spanking, only teaches them that **"might is right"**.

Kids raised by strict parents often face problems with anger and depression later in life. They have learned that something must be "wrong" with them for their parents to treat them so harshly. They miss out on the important lessons of self-regulation and self-control. These children do not learn to think for themselves or to question authority.

They are more likely to give in to peer pressure in their teenage years and get into trouble.

- **Permissive Parenting**

This style of parenting is the exact opposite of strict parenting. Permissive parents tend to give in to the wants of the child because they are afraid of hurting their feelings. Many of these parents also believe that their child will love them more and be better behaved. "**Wrong!**"

Children raised by permissive parents are often labeled as spoiled brats. They tend to throw more temper tantrums than other children. This parenting style, like the strict parent, causes more bad behavior. Children grow up unhappy and because there are no rules they tend to push their parents more.

Children need limits. They thrive on boundaries. With permissive parenting, there are no rules, limits or boundaries. Children are not able to learn self-discipline with this parenting style. These children learn to get what they want through tantrums, whining and threatening their parents. How many of you threatened to hold your breath until your mom gave into to your demands?

Babies' wants and needs are the same. But as your baby grows into a toddler that will change. Most of the time what a toddler wants is harmful to their safety or developmental needs. How many times have you let your toddler stay up after bedtime because you were just too tired to fight with them? This is one of those times when their wants are harmful to their development.

Allowing your toddler to stay up late means less sleep for you. You will have a tired, cranky child to deal with in the morning. But not getting the proper sleep also affects their development. Sleep deprived children are not able to keep up with their peers when it comes to learning. Over time, this leads to lower self-esteem when they cannot do the same tasks that other children do.

Giving into your child's wants will usually come at the expense of someone else. A sibling, yourself, friends or other family members. The child will grow up expecting everyone to give in to her wants and demands. As grownups, we know that the world does not work this way.

> *Children raised by permissive parents have a harder time making friends or sustaining romantic relationships.*

Children without limits do not learn how to handle difficult emotions, like disappointment or sadness. They have learned that their parents will do anything to prevent them from feeling sad. As they grow they will also avoid situations where they might have to face disappointment. Being able to handle difficult emotions is an important part of learning self-esteem and self-discipline.

When a parent does not set age appropriate limits, the child does not learn how to set limits for himself. This lesson is very important for high school and adulthood. The child will not learn how to set or work towards goals. Goals are necessary as they help us to achieve success and happiness in life.

Children of permissive parents tend to find it difficult to internalize happiness. They do not understand that happiness does not come from having all of their wishes fulfilled. They do not have the ability to realize that happiness comes from within. **They may spend their lives looking for the one "thing" they think will make them happy but never find it.**

So if neither of these parenting methods work to raise happy, well-behaved kids, what does? **"Simple, Positive Parenting."** Good parents know how to set appropriate, empathetic limits. They understand that children naturally want to please their parents so that they will love them more.

3 PEACEFUL PARENT, PEACEFUL CHILD

You may have heard of positive parenting by one of its other names. This parenting style is also known as positive guidance, loving guidance or peaceful parenting. Studies have shown that this is the style that works the best to raise happy children who want to behave.

Positive parents use simple guidance, offered in a loving manner, which helps to keep kids on the right track. These parents have learned how to control their own emotions so they do not take them out on their children. Peaceful parents understand how to guide their children depending on their developmental needs.

Loving guidance does not use fear or threats of punishment to make the child behave. These methods of behavior control have been shown to do more harm to a child than good. A positive parent does not yell or say things out of frustration. Any parent can learn positive parenting, it just takes a little time to retrain yourself before you can expect to retrain your child.

One of the first things a parent needs to understand is proper discipline. For generations parents thought this meant some form of physical punishment, like spanking. However, the word discipline comes from the word disciple, which means "to teach". The best way to get your child to behave and keep behaving is to teach them self-discipline. **A child misbehaves for three reasons.** One, the child does not understand what is expected of him. Two, the child knows but cannot control herself. And three, the child knows what is expected but just doesn't care. Let's take a look at how positive parenting can be used in each of these situations.

When the child does not know what is expected it is the parents job to teach them. For example, when your child is young you teach them not to touch the stove because it may be hot. As the child grows you will teach them important lessons like not playing in the street because they could be hit by a car. Or not to talk to or accept candy from strangers.

This type of teaching is also done by modeling. Children learn from watching other people's behavior. When you ask your child to please pick up their toys, they will learn how to say please in return. When you wait for the green light to cross the street, they will learn to do the same.

Understanding childhood developmental milestones is very important. Often parents just expect the child to know better. We tend to forget that we did not teach them an important lesson when we should have. But what happens when the child does know better but misbehaves anyway?

In the reasons why a child misbehaves, we saw that children often do know better but cannot control themselves. In this case we need to teach them how to regulate themselves and self-discipline. Grownups may understand right from wrong but that does not always prevent us from making bad choices. **Children have to learn impulse control.**

The way to learn this is being motivated by, and aware of, competing impulses. For example, as an adult instead of going out with your friends on a work night, you choose to stay home. You know that going out is a bad idea because you do not want to go to work with a hangover. For a child it may look like, I really don't want to do the dishes, I would rather play outside with my friends, but I don't want mom to get mad at me.

Learning how to control our impulses takes a maturity. It comes with time and lessons learned in life. As parents it is our job to help our child learn how to do this. We do it by modeling and by helping them to understand and work through difficult situations.

The best way to do this is to provide your child with experiences where compassion outweighs anger.

When our emotions are heightened it becomes difficult to make wise choices. Yelling at our children only elevates the emotions of our child and ourselves. Positive parenting is about giving you and the child time to calm down. During this time your child will learn how to regulate their emotions and reflect on what they did wrong. Once your child is calm it is easier to work with them to help them to recognize and control their emotions.

What about the child who knows better but just doesn't care? This is a relationship problem not a behavioral problem. Loving guidance will not work with a child who is not willing to receive it. In this case, you need to work on rebuilding the relationship first.

Kids only learn how to regulate themselves and do what we want because they want to please us. This begins in early childhood. When the parent child relationship is nurtured properly, your child will work to please you rather than misbehave and make you angry. The positive parent understands that love is a powerful motivator. Fear and punishment will only work for a little while but will harm your relationship.

Love is the best motivator to make your child want to behave.

4 POSITIVE PARENTING IN ACTION

Now that you know what positive parenting is and why it works best, it's time to put those lessons into action. Changing your parenting style will not be easy at first. It will feel unnatural, and there will be many days when you slip up. Do not be hard on yourself when this happens. Take a breath and remember that it will get easier with practice.

When you transition into being a peaceful parent you will not only heal yourself but your child too. As the old hurts and anger are healed your child will want to listen to you more. As a result you will strengthen your relationship and have more love in your home. Here are the steps to take to put your new parenting plan into action.

1. **Begin with yourself. Peaceful parenting means being a peaceful person.** Do not react when your emotions are running high. Take the time to stop what you are doing and focus on how you are feeling. Take a deep breath and count to ten. Pay attention to the feelings in your body, this will also help you to teach your children to do the same.

This step is not easy and will require a commitment on your part. You will have to commit to taking a time out when you are upset to regulate your emotions. With time and practice it will become a habit. Every time you do this you are building impulse control. This step also helps to remove all of those upsetting triggers so that you will not experience these same emotions in the future.

2. **Focus on your connection with your child.** Positive parenting doesn't work if there is not a strong relationship between you and your child. Start by building that connection. Spend time every day with your child doing something together.

We all lead busy lives but even 15 minutes of quality one-on-one time can go a long way to strengthening your bond.

Missing this step will only lead to failure. When you drop the punishments your child will not be motivated to behave if you have not built this strong connection.

3. **Talk with your child about the new change taking place.** This step will again help to strengthen the bond and encourage your child to take part in the process. The words you use will depend on the age of your child. Your conversation might look like this:

"You know how I use to yell and punish you when you misbehaved? Well, have you noticed that I am yelling a lot less? I am sorry that I used to yell so much. I love you very much and I know that you are trying really hard. I want to help you understand your feelings when you are upset. I think you will learn more from taking care of your mistakes than from me punishing you for them. Let's work together to fix these problems when they happen."

4. **Ask for your child's cooperation.** Explain to them that the rules of the house haven't changed. Tell them that the number one rule is to treat each other with kindness. Make a promise to work not to yell and to be kind, and then ask them to work on this rule too. When your child slips up, as they mostly likely will, do not be too hard on them. Instead model the appropriate behavior you wish to see from them.

5. **Offer support and show them appropriate solutions.** "I know it upsets you when your little brother plays with your dolls. Instead of yelling at him how about we find a safe place to put them so he cannot reach them? When your brother starts to annoy you what else can you do besides yell at him?"

6. **Continue to set age appropriate limits.** As you improve your positive parenting style, you will find yourself becoming more flexible. But remember that children need limits.

   The trick is to set them before you become upset. Empathize with his perspective; "I know you don't want to go to bed right now. When you grow up you will probably stay up playing all night. But right now it is time for bed". Acknowledging their perspective will go a long way towards making your child want to cooperate with you.

7. **Expect emotions to bubble up.** Children that are punished for misbehavior have learned to bottle up the bad feelings that got them into trouble. But we

know that bottled up emotions erupt eventually. Do not take your child's emotional outbursts personally. Often times they do not have the communication skills to express what they are feeling and act out instead.

It is important for you to remember that every behavior is a form of communication. The key here is to help your child understand the emotion behind the misbehavior and to work through it.

8. **Create a safe place.** When your child acts out due to anger or frustration, remember to stay calm. The more compassionate you are the safer your child will feel in expressing their upset feelings with you. Learning to express these emotions, and crying if they feel the need, is healing. Once they get their feelings out and understand them they will be less likely to act out.

9. **Use a story to help your child understand their experience.** Stories help children to understand their emotions. Be careful to keep the story empathic so your child does not feel like they are being lectured to. An example could be: "When you were little I used to yell a lot because I was having a hard time. I didn't know what else to do. I know this scared you and sometimes you would get really mad. But now I work really hard to be nicer and not yell so much. And I know that you are working harder to learn better ways to show me when you are upset. We are learning to solve our problems as a family. When we try to listen and be kind to each other we make things better between us".

10. **Teach your child about reparations.** Once everyone is calmed down, start a discussion with your child about what happened. Remember to empathize with her and listen to her side. Point out the damage that was done by the misbehavior; "when you said that to your little brother it really hurt his feelings". Ask her if there is anything she can do to repair the damage. Do not force her to apologize as this will only feel like a punishment. Teaching your child how to repair the damage they have caused will help them to see that they do not want to act this way again.

11. **Show them how to apologize by modeling.** When you force your child to apologize for a misbehavior, it only causes resentment. But when you take responsibility and apologize for your actions they will learn to do the same.

12. **Expect setbacks.** After all, this new parenting approach is new to you and your child. There will be days when you slip up and the yelling will happen. Forgive yourself and be sure to apologize to your child. It takes time to retrain yourself to a new way of reacting to your child. But don't worry, with time and practice it does get easier.

The next step in practicing positive parenting is understanding how to work with each of the developmental stages of childhood. Toddlers need to learn different lessons than pre-teens. The next few chapters explore the different age groups and how to implement positive parenting for each one.

5 POSITIVE PARENTING FROM DAY ONE

For most people having a baby is an emotional time. You will feel joy, satisfaction and a sense of fulfillment. On the flip side, you will also be tired, cranky and frustrated. The first few weeks are the hardest. Sure you read all the parenting books while you were pregnant, but nothing really prepares you for the day to day work involved with an infant.

The first year of your child's life is one of the most important. How you relate to your baby and the bond you establish now will affect the rest of your lives. Establishing a loving relationship now will pave the way to how your child behaves in the future.

During the year between birth and age one your child's brain is constantly learning. Your baby is learning how to focus her vision and to explore the world around her. Her brain is busy learning cognitive functions like language, memory, thinking and reasoning. She is also learning love and trust which are crucial to social and emotional development.

Begin being a positive parent from day one. Talk to your baby often. He will be comforted by the sound of your voice. When he begins to make sounds of his own, repeat them back to him. Help him to use language by adding words to his babble. Read to him, this will help him to understand words and language and is also a great tool to use for bonding. Studies have shown that music stimulates the brain. Play music and sing to your baby. Singing is another way to help them learn language. As they grow, you can add in dancing to help encourage physical development.

Cuddle and hold your baby often. Doing this will help them to feel safe and loved. Children that start out feeling safe grow up to be more competent later in life. Praise her for accomplishing developmental tasks. The more loving attention you give her now, the more she will want to please you later.

Spend time playing with your baby when they are alert. Be sure to give him a break if he begins to get tired or fussy. As he grows you can use toys and playtime to distract him from things that he should not be doing. Such as wandering into the kitchen while you are cooking.

And take the time to take care of you. This cannot be stressed enough. Parenting is hard work. If you are not well rested frustration can rear its ugly head and get the best of you. Positive parents know it is important to take care of their needs as well as their child's needs.

Happy parents tend to raise happy children.

6 TERRIFIC TWOS AND BEYOND

Many parents, call this childhood stage the terrible twos. But your toddler is learning new skills almost daily. And they are changing right before your eyes. **I would say that is terrific.** Your child should hit many new milestones in the years between one and three. Please remember that these are average. If your child takes a little longer than others, do not get upset. Most children will learn at their own pace.

Between the ages of one and two your darling baby will begin to walk. She will also start saying simple words like "mama" and "dada". She will be more active and become more aware of herself and her surroundings. She is starting to explore the world around her and trying to make sense of it.

Many parents find this stage to be rather difficult. Gone are the days when you knew where your baby was at all times. Now he is everywhere including places you do not want him to be. During this stage, he should be able to recognize himself in a mirror and will begin to imitate the actions of those around him.

Your toddler may also start to become more defiant. This is the perfect time to begin setting those boundaries. A good place to start is with a regular routine. When your child knows what is coming next, it is easier for her to adjust. A daily routine helps them to learn to make sense of the world. Between the ages of two and three your child will start to become more independent. Your toddler will begin to learn social skills, like taking turns. You should be seeing some imaginary play. Physical skills may include kicking a ball or jumping in place. All of these are necessary for them to be able to explore their world more.

Their little brains are learning all the time. Toddlers will start to be able to follow simple directions, no more than three steps at a time. He should be able to sort items by colors and shapes. And you will also see a new range of emotions. All of these changes are exciting and normal. **But these little people will test the limits of your patience. Remember they are learning new skills at a rapid pace.**

Make time to read to your toddler every day. A good time for this is before bedtime. Make it part of her nightly routine. This will help to eliminate tantrums when she does not want to go to bed. And it will help her to learn to transition between daytime and nighttime.

Work with your toddler to encourage their language development. Make playtime fun and educational. You can have him name all of his body parts. Ask him to find objects or toys you have placed around the house. And this is a good time to start teaching them matching games. When you child says a simple word, like "baba", add to that, "Yes, that is a bottle".

Your toddler will want to do more things by themselves. Encourage that by letting them dress themselves. You will find that toddlers have an interesting fashion sense. **Go ahead and let them wear the cowboy boots with their pajamas. It won't hurt anyone and will help their developing self-esteem.**

She will also be learning how to feed herself. During this age many children develop rather picky eating habits. Do not worry when your toddler does not want to eat when you want her to. Toddlers do not need as much food as babies because their growth process has slowed down. Let her explore new tastes and textures.

Praise the good behavior and ignore the bad. When your child is doing something good, like playing nicely with his toys, tell him so. Letting your child know when they are good will encourage them to continue being good. Try to ignore the bad behavior.

At this age, many children start to throw tantrums when they do not get their way. The child is not trying to be bad. She just doesn't have the language skills to tell you how she feels yet. The only way she knows to express her anger or unhappiness is with a tantrum. If you do not pay attention, the behavior will cease. After all it is no fun making a scene if no one is there to witness it.

Remember that positive parenting only works if there is a strong bond between you and your child. Many parents use the television or computer to keep their kids entertained. At this age, your child should not be exposed to any media. Make the time to play with and interact with your child.

Establish a loving connection with you, not the television!

7 THE MAGIC YEARS

Preschool includes the ages between three and five. This childhood stage is often referred to as the magic years. You will find that your child's imagination knows no bounds. **To them, everything is new and exciting and full of wonder. Many parents try to discourage this creative thinking; please do not be one of those.**

Your child will begin to tell you fantastical stories. At this age, many children develop imaginary friends. Do not be concerned, they are not crazy. Imagination in a child should be encouraged, not squashed. When they get out into the world, they will learn soon enough that the world can be a harsh place.

Also during this time you will notice that your child may be more affectionate. They will enjoy spending time just cuddling with you. Use this cuddle time to strengthen your bond and make sure to enjoy every minute of it. **Too soon they will be making friends outside the home and no longer want to play with you.**

Preschoolers will start to take a bigger interest in the world outside the home. They will begin to ask questions about how and why things work. **"Why is the sky blue, or the grass green" are quite common**. Encourage this exploration with field trips to the park or a walk in the woods. Continue to develop your child's love of books by introducing them to the library. Together you can find the answers to all of their questions. Let your child collect rocks, or leaves or whatever interests them.

Children will also be more physically active during this stage. They should be able to ride a tricycle, with adult supervision. At this age, you should begin conversations about safety. Explain why they shouldn't ride their tricycle in the street. Start teaching them about strangers and why they should never get in their cars and accept things from them.

Your child will be interested in playing with other children. Socialization is important because it teaches your child lessons like sharing and friendship. At this age, they will also realize there is a difference between boys and girls. Be prepared to answer their questions and explain the differences.

Support their growing independence by giving them simple chores. You should pick no more than two to start with. Have him dust the living room tables, or pick up his toys before bed. Keep it simple but make sure to praise him for a job well done so he will want to keep it up. Another fun idea is to let them help in the kitchen. Spending time baking or helping with dinner is another way to connect with your child while teaching them new skills.

Strengthen their growing vocabulary and language skills. Be sure to use "grownup" words when speaking to them. Also use full sentences now. When it comes to disciplining them be consistent and explain to them why the behavior is unacceptable. Continue to praise them for their good behaviors. Make sure you are modeling the behavior you want to see in your child.

At this age, you can start to expose your child to media. Be sure to limit it to no more than two hours a day. Monitor what your child is watching and discuss it with them. Keep the shows, or video games, age appropriate and educational if possible. But remember, media devices should never take away from quality family time.

8 OH THE PLACES THEY WILL GO, LIKE SCHOOL

Early childhood covers the ages of six to eight. By this time, your child is going to school. He is being exposed to new ideas by his teachers and his peers. This can be a frightening time for parents. You are no longer in control of what he learns or sees all of the time. He may come home from school with new words that are not appropriate or ideas that you may not approve of.

During this stage, you will see a big change in social and emotional skills. Your child is beginning to form friendships with other people outside of the family. She is starting to think about her future and her place in the world. She will develop more independence and have a greater need to be liked by her peers.

Between six and eight your child will also show changes in how he thinks and learns. Children this age develop a rapid growth in mental skills. He will be able to solve more complex problems on his own. Your child should also be better able to understand and talk about his feelings. His focus will shift from thinking about himself to being more considerate of others. Continue to strengthen your bond by showing affection. Praise them for their accomplishments. Spend time doing things as a family. If you haven't established a dinner routine now is the time. Make it rule to sit down together and talk about their day. Ask them about school, what they learned, what activities they are interested in, etc. Dinner time should also be a time of no television or cell phones allowed at the table.

You should make a habit of spending at least 15 minutes a day talking to your child. Ask them about their friends. What plans do they have for their future? This time can also be used to talk about things like responsibility, any problems they may be having in school or at home. If you establish open communication when they are young, they will be more likely to talk to you when they reach the difficult teenage years.

At this age children should be given more responsibility around the house. Set up a chore chart or routine so they know what is expected of them. Help them to learn the value of teamwork. Show them that by working together you can get more accomplished and have more time for fun.

Continue setting clear, age-appropriate boundaries. Make sure they understand what the rules are. Decide how long they can watch TV and what chores need to be done before they can go outside to play. Try not to make the focus on all of the things they should not do, but talk about the positive things to do instead. Avoid punishing bad behavior and be sure to praise the good things they are doing.

Teach them how to set achievable goals. When they work to get something they want it will mean more to them. This lesson will be extremely valuable to them later in life. You will help them to develop both self-esteem and self-discipline which are necessary for them to want to be good.

Stay involved in your child's life. This doesn't mean that you need to know every single thing they are doing every minute of the day. Get involved with their school. Meet the teacher and find out what curriculum they are following.

Get your child involved in community activities. Sign them up for after school activities that are supervised. Use this to teach them patience, caring and tolerance. Show them how to care for others in need.

A good way to do this is to have them go through their toys before the holidays. Throw out the broken ones and gather up the ones they no longer play with. Take them to one of the local shelters and let them give their toys to a child in need. Let them see how a simple act of kindness can change a person's life.

9 IS IT TIME FOR "THE TALK"

As your child starts to approach puberty, you will notice some significant emotional and social changes. Middle childhood covers the ages of 9 to 11. At this stage, they are becoming more interested in what their peer group thinks of them. It becomes very important for them to have strong friendships with the same sex. You will find they are less interested in spending time with you and more interested in other activities.

Your child will also become more aware of her body. Body image and how others see her will be more important. For many young girls, this is when eating disorders begin to develop. If you have been helping her to develop a strong self-esteem she will be less likely to be influenced by her peers.

Children this age also experience changes in how they think and learn. They are able to take on more challenging work at school. Their attention span is longer. They are now able to see other people's point of view. They are becoming more mature and developing the ability to empathize with others.

Keep talking. But don't just talk at your child, stop and listen too. Ask them questions. Let them tell you how they feel or what they are thinking. Now is a good time to help them expand on goal setting. Don't just focus on a "thing" they want but find out what kinds of skills they want to learn. Show them how to accomplish this.

Continue to recognize their accomplishments at school and around the house. Give them more responsibility. Don't just tell her how proud you are of her. Be sure to say things like "you must be really proud of yourself". This will encourage her to make good choices even when you are not around.

Now is the time to begin "the talk". This topic makes many a parent squirm. But unless you want your child to learn about sex from a stranger, or worse their friends, you need to take a deep breath and go. At this age, the talk does not need to focus on sex itself. Instead, talk to them about the changes they are experiencing.

Teach them about puberty. Let them know what to expect. Explain to them all of the changes their bodies will go through. Be sure to also let them know that what they are going through. Puberty is such a confusing time for a child. But giving them a "safe" place to talk about it will make it easier.

Another topic for conversation is risky behavior. Help your child to develop his sense of right and wrong. Talk to him about peer pressure. Explain to him what risky behavior is. This includes topics like smoking, drinking alcohol, ditching school and trying drugs. Tell him about the consequences that come from doing these things. Ask him questions to make sure he understands.

Continue to teach your child about responsibility. Teach them about money management. Give them optional chores they can do around the house to earn a little money. Teach them the importance of saving money. Explain to them about working for a wage.

For example, your child asks you for the newest game system that just came out. The game costs $300 and you make $12 an hour. Show them how many hours you have to work to earn that extra $300.

This will help them to develop an appreciation of money.

10 WHERE DID MY HAPPY CHILD GO?

Ugh, it's here, adolescence. For both the parent and the child, this can be the most difficult stage to get through. Adolescence covers the ages of 12 – 14. Your happy child turns into a moody, secretive stranger. So many complex emotional and social changes begin to develop.

At this age, they are more focused on themselves. They are likely to go through extremes, having high expectations one moment and suffering from a complete lack of confidence the next. The focus becomes all about their bodies, how they look and what clothes to wear.

Being liked and accepted by their peers is of the upmost importance. During this stage, they are also more likely to give in to peer pressure than ever before. Your once loving child no longer seems to care about what you think. He may be rude, dismissive and short tempered with you. Understand that adolescence brings with it stress, sadness and depression.

Keep the lines of communication open. Talk to your teen and ask them questions. Try not to ask open-ended questions that can be answered with a yes or no. If you did not cover the topic of sex and risky behavior before, do so now. Make sure your child knows the consequences for such behavior; like teen pregnancy or juvenile detention. Stay involved in your child's life. This is critical right now. Get to know their friends and their parents. Stay involved with their school. Go to school activities or games. Get them involved in sports or community activities. A busy child has less time to get into trouble.

Do things as a family, even when they do not want to. If you established a family game night, then continue with this. Find activities that are fun for everyone. Maybe do a movie night once a week and take turns picking out what to see. Then talk about the movie together.

Help your child learn how to make healthy choices. Be sure that you continue to model the type of behavior that you want her to learn. An adolescent's feelings are easily hurt so be sure to choose your words wisely when discussing their bodies, friends or actions.

Keep recognizing their accomplishments. Set reasonable boundaries about what you expect and let them help with those decisions. Don't do all of the talking. Encourage your teenager to talk about his feelings and share his thoughts. Be respectful of what they tell you. Try to remember what it was like when you were a teenager. What kind of restrictions did your parents put on you that you hated? What made you rebel against them? What things did your parents do that worked to help you develop a good self-esteem?

11 MY BABY IS ALL GROWNUP

So you survived adolescence, yeah for you. As a parent, you are now in the home stretch. The teenage years cover the ages of 15 – 17. Your beautiful little baby is almost an adult. As a parent, you need to begin to treat him like one. They are still growing, learning and changing and need you to guide them.

At this age it becomes more important what peers of the opposite sex think. Make sure to talk to them about sex and dating. Teach them how to handle themselves in difficult situations. For example, if they are being pressured to have sex, or why they shouldn't get in the car of a friend who has been drinking.

Teenagers are under a lot of pressure to "fit in". You will notice your teen going through bouts of sadness and depression. If you are noticing big changes in the way they act, dress or the friends they hang out with, talk to them and ask them how they feel, so you know if they have any stress or depression that can lead them to hurt themselves. Knowing that they can talk to you about their feelings may just save their life.

Talk to your teenager about the dangers of social media. Be aware of what sites they are visiting on the internet. Have a discussion with them to make them aware of what they should or should not post. Teach them about internet predators and the dangers of sharing personal information with someone they do not know.

Your teenager will be thinking more about her future. What happens after high school? What kind of job does she want? Does she want to go to college? Does she want to get married and have a family? Make sure you discuss these topics with her. **Help her to set goals to accomplish her future plans.**

Give your teenager more responsibility. Encourage them to get a part-time job. Every teenager dreams of having their own car. Help them to set a goal to make this happen. Take them to one of the local used car lots and let them look around.

This gives them to chance to have a realistic idea of what a car costs. You might consider offering to match them for the cost. If they have to work and save for the car they will be more likely to be responsible while driving it.

Respect your teenager's need for privacy. This can be a difficult task for many parents. Your teen will be pulling away from the family more as she prepares herself for adulthood. She will be less interested in family activities and spend more time with friends. As a parent, if you do not want to damage the bond you have built, you will need to learn to respect her privacy and give her space.

That doesn't mean you should stop talking. Oh no. Continue communicating all the time. But remember to listen to her thoughts and feelings too. Good communication will help her to make good choices.

And do be honest with your child when they ask you a question. Even when the question makes you uncomfortable. Gone are the days when a parent could just make up an answer to a question. Today's kids have the internet.

If you have formed a loving relationship with your child, getting through the teen years should not be too difficult. Being a positive parent from the start will have helped your child to build a strong foundation for their future.

They should have a healthy self-esteem so that they do not give in to the demands of their peers. They will have formed a sense of self-discipline that will help them to make good choices. And you will have a strong family bond that will carry you into the future.

12 TIPS TO BE A MORE POSITIVE PARENT

When it comes to parenting, we either repeat what we know or do the exact opposite. If your parents yelled at you, you are more likely to yell at your child. Or you will remember how much you hated that and decide not to yell before your child is even born. If you want to stop the yelling and become a more peaceful parent you need to start by changing you.

When you make the decision to become a positive parent you are not just healing your relationship with your child. **You will heal yourself too. Most of us consider ourselves to be good parents. We would never do anything to intentionally harm our child. But the truth is that most of us were wounded in some way when we were children.**

To be a peaceful parent we need to heal these old wounds. If we do not, we are likely to harm our own children in the same way. This is not intentional by any means, it is just part of what becomes a never ending cycle. We need to take the time to lovingly parent ourselves in the same way we do our children.

You can use these six steps to begin your healing process.

1. **Be a conscience parent.** Learn to recognize your "triggers" and deal with them. When your child does something that makes you exceptionally angry, realize that this anger is coming from an old wound of yours. Figure out what caused this wound and then you can begin to heal it.

2. **You can break the cycle.** Think about how your parents hurt you and realize that you are on the same path. Stop! When you feel an outburst coming on, walk out of the room. Remind yourself that you are modeling good anger management skills.

3. **Understand how anger works.** Anger is a biological reaction that stimulates the "fight or flight" response. This heightened state makes anyone, even your child, look like the enemy. Too often anger causes us to say and do things we would not do otherwise.

4. **Rewrite your story.** You cannot change the past. What you can do is change how it affects you now. If you felt like it was your fault because your parents got divorced see the situation threw your grownup eyes. As an adult you understand that it was not you but they just couldn't get along. Rewriting your childhood story is very liberating. Know that you can be the parent you want to be.

5. **Eliminate stress.** Doing this is not always an easy thing. Adults lead stressful lives and parents even more so. Take time for you. Do the activities that help

you to relieve stress. Exercise, take a walk, lock yourself in the bathroom and soak in a hot bubble bath. If you find it impossible to get alone time, then make it a family activity.

6. **Get help when you need it.** Asking for help does not make you weak. Part of being a mature adult is knowing when to seek help. Check for parent support groups in your area. Being around other people who are going through the same things as you can work wonders. You will realize that you are not alone.

10 Steps to Stop the Yelling

1. Your first job as a parent is to keep your child safe. Your second job is to manage your own emotions. Remember that children learn by observing those around them. When you learn to control your emotions they will learn by modeling.

2. Make a commitment, out loud, to your family that you will use a kinder voice. Let them know that you are trying and you will make some mistakes but you will get better with practice.

3. Remember that kids are kids. They are immature little beings without the means to control their own emotions. Kids don't think straight when they are upset.

4. Don't let resentments build up. We all do this, especially when we are having a bad day. It may have started at work where your boss yelled at you for something a coworker did. As the day progresses, those resentments build up until you explode. Take a time out to deal with these emotions. Do something

that makes you feel better.

5. When your child expresses an emotion show them empathy. The first step in learning to control emotions is to accept them. Once your child has learned how to manage their emotions they can then manage their behavior.

6. Establish that connection with your child and see things from their perspective. Your child needs to know that you understand them and are on their side. A child is more willing to behave when they have a loving relationship with their parent.

7. **When you get angry don't say another word. Don't make any decisions out of anger. Stop what you are doing and just breathe. Don't take any action until you feel calm again.**

8. When anger rears its ugly head, try to remove yourself from the situation. If this is not possible, do something, anything, that help you shift your focus from your child to your feelings. Find what is under the anger, it may be fear, sadness or disappointment. Feel that real feeling, cry if you need to, and the anger will dissolve.

9. Find your inner guiding angel. Imagine you have a guiding angel on your shoulder. What advice would she give in this situation? What would she tell you to do to make things better?

10. Choose a plan of action from this calm place. You might need to apologize to your child. Or this could mean holding her while she cries it out. Or just spend

some time playing together until you both feel better.

Please be sure you do not set your expectations too high. No parent is perfect. Humans, by their very nature, are imperfect creatures. And that's OK. Here are nine tips you can use to be a better parent.

1. Work to build your child's self-esteem. We have talked about this in previous chapters but it cannot be stressed enough. One of the best ways to raise a happy child that wants to behave is by building their self-esteem. Choose your words carefully. Make sure not to compare them with their siblings or say things that will make them feel bad about themselves. Recognize and praise their accomplishments, even the little ones.

2. Make an effort to catch your kids being good. Too often we tend to see the bad behaviors and focus on them. This leads to a lot of negativity, in our words and actions, throughout the day. Make a habit of noticing when your kids are being good and praise them for it.

3. Be consistent. So very important. If bedtime is 8:00 then make sure they are ready to go by 8:00. If one of the house rules is not TV until the homework is done, make sure this happens. When parents give in to the rules they set, kids will be confused and naturally try to push the limits.

4. Make time for your kids. Plan a family night once a week and let the kids help decide what you will be doing. Get up a little early so you have time to eat breakfast with them. Drop by their school and have lunch with them if you can. Put a note in their lunchbox letting them know you love them. Kids will

remember these little things when they grow up.

5. Be the person you want your kids to be. Say please and thank-you. Help other people without expecting anything in return. Give sincere compliments when they are deserved. Your kids are watching you and will model the behavior they see in you.

6. Communication is important. Your kids need more from you than "because I said so". When they come to with questions answer them honestly. Nothing will destroy the loving connection you are building faster than lying to them. Remember, they have access to computers and internet and can find answers for themselves. Make time to talk to your kids about what they are doing every day.

7. Be flexible and adjust according to their developmental needs. Just because a book says a child should be potty trained by two, does not mean that all children will be. Small children need your supervision while older children need time to play with their friends or to be by themselves.

8. Show your children unconditional love. Even when confrontations happen handle them in a loving, nurturing way. Talk to your children, not at them. Give them time to express their thoughts and feelings. And let them know that you will love them no matter what.

9. Know your strengths and weaknesses. A strength may be that you are good at organization. Your house is always neat and clean and everything in its place. A weakness may be that you need to be more consistent

with setting limits.

Know that being a parent is the hardest job in the world. Being a parent is also the most rewarding. *Do not stress over getting it perfect. None of us do.* Make a conscious effort to be a positive parent and you will be on the right track. Work every day on creating a loving connection and open communication.

And be as good to yourself when you slip up as you are to your kids. In no time at all you will have achieved peaceful parenting and created a home full of love.

Copyright and Disclaimer

All rights reserved. Without limiting the rights under copyright reserved above, no part of this publication maybe reproduced, stored in or introduced into a retrieval system, or transmitted in any form, or by any means (electronic, mechanical, photocopying, recording or otherwise) without the prior written permission of both the copyright owner and the publisher of this book.

ABOUT THE AUTHOR

For me, the hardest part of being a mom is learning how to manage my own emotions. After having a baby, I found myself yelling at my husband and my son every day, I felt horrible and guilty afterward, and I felt so stressed and tired all the time.

I started reading lots of self-help books and I have learned a lot. Now, I feel happier, positive and relaxed and I stopped yelling.

I want to share what I have learned throughout the years with my readers; I hope my books can help you deal with your day-to-day challenges, and make you feel happy again, you can create a home full of peace and love for the whole family.

Motivational Quotes:

http://improve-yourself-today.com/motivational-quotes-page/

Made in the USA
Middletown, DE
10 August 2022